JESS

THE SHOCK OF A LIFETIME

BY:

JESSE SINK

THE SHOCK OF A LIFETIME

Copyright © 2018 by JESSE SINK

All rights reserved. No part of this publication may be reproduced, distributed, or transmitted in any form or by any means, including photocopying, recording, or other electronic or mechanical methods, without the prior written permission of the author, except in the case of brief quotations embodied in critical reviews and certain other noncommercial uses permitted by copyright law.

Ordering Information:
Quantity sales. Special discounts are available on quantity purchases by corporations, associations, and others.
Orders by U.S. trade bookstores and wholesalers.
Please contact JESSE SINK via www.BionicJesse.com

Edited and Marketed By
DreamStarters University
www.DreamStartersUniversity.com

JESSE SINK

Table of Contents

Tiger in a Cage 6

Call From the Universe 16

The Shock of a Lifetime 22

The Gates of Heaven 28

Time Passed Without Me 34

The Second Shock 40

Fighting Back 46

Help on the Road to Recovery 52

Nothing to Lose 58

A Force to Be Reckoned With 64

Go All the Way 70

I'm Not Them 76

Don't Settle for "No" 82

Magic Out of Pain 88

Setbacks are Temporary 95

Be an Unrealistic Fighter 102

Photo Gallery 107

About Jesse Sink 112

THE SHOCK OF A LIFETIME

Thank you to my family and friends for being there when I needed you most.

The one thing I never did was let myself be a victim of a situation that happened FOR me. I created my reality by what I thought and believed. So I needed to take responsibility and learn to grow. – Jesse Sink

"What you think, you will create."

JESSE SINK

Chapter 1

Tiger in a Cage

We are all born with greatness inside us. Some of us realize this earlier than others and some never see it at all. My journey to where I am now has been a series of ups and downs. As you will see in this book, losing my arm and being burned alive in a tragic accident has not defined my life. It is only a part of my journey. The people I have met, the places I have gone, and the obstacles I have overcome because of it have given me a perspective I would not have otherwise.

There is a thought that that we actually choose the families were born into. If you had a wonderful childhood, you might agree with that thinking. Yet if you were born into families like many of us, where our parents were doing the best they knew how yet carried the values and instructions manual that was handed to them by their you may seriously question that thinking.

We sometimes experience generations of pain, struggles and not knowing what we don't know. Hey, there's no instruction manual for life and parenting. When your innate instincts are so strong and the knowing of who you are, the world might not open its arms to welcome you.

I knew early on I was hard wired for speed. From drag racing, sports biking, street racing and high speed stunting I loved the thrill of it. I knew I had something unique within me that was powerful and bigger than the circumstances I was born into. In many ways I was the tiger in a cage. There was greatness that felt confined by my surroundings and circumstances.

Little did I know that the tiger would be unleash by a twist of faith that took me to the other side of death and beyond. It is that experience that I share with you through my story. I cleared the depths of despair to experiencing a life of inspiration. That did not happen for me to keep myself in a cage but to share with you and the world in hopes that in some small or big way your life is touched in a positive manner. May you find strength you didn't know you had to breakthrough any cages or barriers that prevent you from living your best life.

I take you back to my humble beginning to go forward together into endless possibilities. I currently live in California, but my story began in an unlikely place—on a farm. Growing up, I felt like I was a wild tiger being kept in a cage. I grew up in a very conservative family, and this was very difficult for me. I saw everyone around me having fun and enjoying life, but in the simplest terms, I felt trapped. There was nothing I could do to escape. When I finally got out into the wild, it was hard for me to adjust. Most people living a "normal lifestyle" don't go through the adjustment period I had to go through when I left my parents' home. I didn't have a bad family life growing up. My parents raised me with the tools they had and I am extremely appreciative of the love and care my parents expressed.

    I was raised on a farm, where we learned the essence of hard work. My dad was one of the hardest working men I've known. He ran the farm, and he was truly a jack-of-all-trades. My dad did whatever needed to be done, from carpentry to plumbing. He grew up differently than a lot of people do, and I owe a lot of my abilities to what he taught me.

    He wanted a big family, so he and my mom had eight children. I'm the middle child. Every Sunday I went to church with my family, and I lived a peaceful life surrounded by a lot of good people, but I felt something was missing all along.

    Something wasn't right. Everybody outside of my immediate family and church friends always questioned why my family lived the way we did. We lived a very simple life. If you've seen the TV show Breaking Amish, it's a show that I find relates to my life very closely.

Looking back, I'm grateful for my upbringing, but it challenged me to my core. Some things about the way we lived I just didn't understand. We weren't allowed to have a TV or a radio in the house. It was crazy, but I wasn't even allowed to wear a t-shirt with lettering on it. And if I didn't cut my hair, I would have gotten kicked out of the house.

My father had very high standards. He had a lot of rules. They were not all bad. He meant well, and it was hard for my father to understand any other ways of life that were much different than the German Baptist upbringing he had. I'm not saying his way of life wasn't good. It's just that it was not God's plan for me to continue in it. This is what frustrated me in my younger years. My brothers and sisters struggled with the same things I did, but I especially wanted to experience more of the world.

I enjoyed being around the cows and pigs and everything on the farm, but I wanted to do something bigger with my life. I had a burning desire to experience more than the small town, farming lifestyle. I felt like something was way off, and I was depressed where I was. I felt out of place and stuck in a rut.

As a young kid, I was embarrassed to be around my parents. When I walked around with them in public, I would hide behind them. I remember thinking to myself back then, "I just wish we were normal." It seemed to me like in our family, we were always worrying about things that didn't REALLY matter. I didn't care if I looked completely clean cut all the time. And, honestly, I didn't feel well at times. It took all I had to get out of bed at 6am every morning to do chores every single day, but that was part of the program at home. I had to play the part of the clean-cut, well-mannered farm boy all the time, whether I liked it or not.

I always wondered why we had to fight and bicker about things like what my pants or shirt looked like. I understood what it meant to be a good, kind human being that showed love to other people. The other parts of my conservative, church-going upbringing I didn't think were necessary. It was all too controlled and strict for me.

At 13 years old, I got my first job off of my parents' farm. I didn't choose the job myself. What happened was a church friend called my mom, and he told her they had some work for me. The job was to pressure wash manure at their farm, and they were going to pay me six bucks an hour.

At the time, I had a friend who was making eight bucks an hour, so I was disappointed with the offer. But I wasn't given the choice to not take the job, and there were other areas of my life that functioned the same way. My parents decided almost everything for me, and there was no arguing with their decisions. It was very clear to me that I wasn't allowed to go to public school. All of the kids in my family went to private school, which was a blessing, but I wanted to play basketball and football. I couldn't do that because my family didn't want me to be influenced by the public.

I now get why they made these decisions. **They loved me.** They didn't want me to be around people who might cause me to get hurt or to get in trouble. But I wanted to be allowed to experience things, and to be guided along the way—not just held back because of my parents' fears. I had an amazing father and mother, and I had an amazing guidance system in the form of a higher power I call God. What was missing was my freedom to learn through my own experience and make my own choices.

When I turned 18 years old, I was finally given the authority to make my own decisions. I got a full-time job and a car. I moved into a little apartment with a friend in town. My family and church didn't approve of the move. They saw it as a form of rebellion.

I started drag racing a 5.0LHO built Ford Mustang that was fast enough to pull wheelies. 160 miles per hour came really fast. (I have busy guardian angels, I think!) My love for racing started at age 12 on a 4 wheeler, now I was racing cars at 18!

THE SHOCK OF A LIFETIME

At 19, I took a job in construction, and I moved to Florida because I was tired of living in a cold climate. I knew construction wasn't what I wanted to do forever, but when I got to Florida, all I could do was let out a sigh of relief. I could finally breathe.

One of the first things I did was I bought a GSXR 600 sport bike. I started street racing and high-speed stunting. I would ride wheelies at 150 miles per hour, topping out at 190 miles per hour. I was good at it, and I got a huge adrenaline rush out of doing this kind of thing. Until I ended up crashing my sport bike. I hit a wet spot on the road going around a turn. I hit a tree head on at 95mph, breaking it off four feet above the ground and sending me 100 feet into a cornfield. I spent the following three days in the ICU.

At that point, I realized I needed to be careful. I was becoming an adrenaline junkie. I left Florida and my daredevil ways behind, and I moved to Indianapolis, Indiana where I got a job working for another construction crew.

While working on the construction crew, I started to dream. I kept thinking about how I wanted to do something that would inspire people. Even as a kid, this is what I wanted to do with my life. I would always pray and say, "God, I want to be someone unique. I want to be someone different. I want to be someone that can inspire people. Give me strength, and show me how to do that."

I didn't know what I was doing when I prayed this prayer as a kid. **But it's now painfully beautiful to me.** What you think and believe within yourself, you will create, so be careful what you wish for. This prayer has set the course for much of life in a lot of ways, and it hasn't been an easy journey to decode. But it has been unique, incredibly challenging, and I hope inspiring for you who are about to read the harrowing story of how I became the man who survived 13,800 volts.

Shock Your Life Into Action

If you are like me, then you know what it's like to feel like a tiger in a cage. I felt trapped early on, and I wanted more out of life. I've had a burning desire to become someone unique and different since childhood. I've always wanted to be able to inspire people to live an amazing life. I've committed to seeing that vision come to life, but it has not been easy. **Your challenges will not be the same as mine, but what you will take away from this book is there is nothing in life you can't overcome. Nothing.** It's time for you to break out and let the world see what has been caged for far too long.

"Never become a victim of your circumstances; things happen in life for you, not to you. Attitude is everything!"

JESSE SINK

Chapter 2

Call From the Universe

While working construction in Indiana, I received a call from a modeling talent scout agency called ProScout. They told me to come try out for a modeling opportunity in New York. The only modeling work I did at that point was for Abercrombie and Hollister as a door model for a short time. Never anything serious.

I've always loved to lift weights and stay in shape. I've been lifting and working on my own health and fitness since I was 13 years old. My father never understood my obsession with lifting weights. We've never seen eye to eye about it.

He always told me, "If you want to get bigger, throw some hay bales, and work out on the farm." I understood his logic, but I've always found weight lifting to be therapeutic. I needed a healthy outlet like lifting when I was kid, because I was depressed and frustrated often. Many times growing up, my mom took me to the doctor for this reason, and they put me on anti-depressants. But for me, workouts were a much better form of a mood enhancement than pills. The gym has never let me down. I always feel and look better after a workout!

As a natural result of my hard work in the gym, I built the perfect body for modeling. So when the talent scout called, I jumped at the opportunity that was being offered to go to New York and present myself to the top 50 modeling agencies in the world. When it was all said and done, I was chosen by one of them. I moved to New York a year later. It was a huge change for me, but I embraced it with all the energy I could muster.

I started working for some big name brands, and I felt like I was moving up the ladder pretty quickly. I did runway shows, and I worked with some very reputable companies very closely. It was a big deal to me, a guy who grew up on a farm who didn't feel like he was worth anything.

Finally, I had a sense of purpose, and I enjoyed what I was doing. I was actually having fun with my work for the first time in my life. I also did high-end catering at a penthouse suite in New York on the side to support myself as I built my modeling career.

THE SHOCK OF A LIFETIME

Although I was doing something I enjoyed, it was difficult for me to adjust to the demands of the modeling industry. A lot of the models had different values than I did. I was raised so much differently than most of them. I did my best to fit in to the scene and meet the right people, but I wasn't totally comfortable with everything.

Some of the ways they wanted to take pictures of me disturbed me. As my career began to take off, I was forced to try to keep everything in balance. I had to try to figure out what I thought was right and what I thought was wrong. I really didn't know. The contrast between my former life on a farm living a conservative, religious lifestyle and my life as a model in New York City was drastic.

But I was determined to figure it out. I was so miserable with my former life, so I decided I'd rather be dead than not go after my dreams. I decided that even if it was going to destroy me, I was going to try to make it work. I figured if God loved me, he'd keep me around even if I made mistakes.

I searched for balance, but it was hard to find. I went out drinking with friends. I did a bump of coke here and there. I wasn't abusing these things, but I didn't live the healthiest lifestyle. I just had no idea what direction I was headed in. I was 21 years old, and I had a lot to learn. I felt more alive than ever before, but I was searching for something solid to ground me.

On the night of my accident, I was working my catering job serving very wealthy people drinks off of trays I balanced effortlessly with one hand. On one of my breaks, I went out on the balcony and called my friend Malinda. I told her, "Hey, I love you. You're my best friend, and I want to let you know I'm happier than I've been in a long time. I miss you. It's hard to do this all alone, but I want you to know I'm going to keep moving forward, and I appreciate you."

When I got off the phone, I watched people down on the ice rink happily skating around in circles. It was cold night, but there's a good reason they call New York City "the city that never sleeps." Everywhere I looked there were people going about their business just like any ordinary night.

I went back inside, and I finished the rest of my shift. By the time we got things packed up, it was already almost three in the morning. I didn't know it at the time, but my night was just beginning. What was to come would change my life forever.

Shock Your Life Into Action

When I was young and just venturing out on my own, I didn't know very well how to navigate the world. I took a lot of risks because I was trying to find out who I was. I went from living within the standards of extreme conservatism to experiencing total freedom. For me, the changes I went through were dramatic, but through them I was learning the importance of being a grounded and well-balanced individual. For once in my life, I was beginning to become established on my own terms. Life though, had a different plan. **Someone or something is calling for you.** You might not want to answer. You might not be ready. You might think it's a mistake. But, there are no mistakes when you listen to your heart, only painful steps. **There is a purpose to it all.**

"Someone or something is calling for you."

JESSE SINK

Chapter 3

The Shock of a Lifetime

One of my catering co-workers looked at me and asked, "Are you doing okay?" I must have looked tired, which was to be expected since I had just finished a long shift, and it was now very late at night. I answered him, "Yeah, I'm good. I'm just going to head home."

He didn't let me go that easy. He asked me, "You want to come out for a drink or two at the bar with my friends and I on the way to the subway?" I was exhausted. I had no interest in going out. I told him I just wanted to get to Penn Station, get on the train and go home to sleep. But he ended up talking me into going out to the bar where we had a couple of drinks together. About six of his friends also joined us at the bar.

Before long, I realized they were all flirting with me, and I became uncomfortable. I'm a straight guy. I tried to respect all these guys, but they were making me feel uneasy. I got weird vibes from them, and I decided I didn't want anything to do with the whole situation, so I nicely told my friend, "I'm out. I need to go to the train."

Everybody begged me to stay, but the energy was weird. I knew something was off, so I told everyone I was leaving, and I ran off towards Penn Station. When I got to Penn Station, that's when things went sideways. Literally.

I started to feel like somebody had given me a shot of morphine. I looked up at the screens to see where my train was at, and everything around me went out of focus. The only thing I could comprehend that was going on in my own head was that I was trying to get to my train. All of my other thoughts were half-formed and extremely confusing.

I rubbed my head. I could not figure out what was going on. I was a 6'2", 200 pound guy at the time, but I was totally wrecked. It felt like I'd drank 10 shots of vodka at the bar, which I definitely hadn't. Someone must have roofied me at the bar. I've never been able to prove this, but there's simply no other explanation.

I tried to stumble my way down the steps to my train, but I could barely steady myself without grabbing on to the handrail. I faded in and out of consciousnesses as my body tried to fight off whatever drug had been slipped into my drink. Gathering myself together as much as possible, I headed off into the direction of the train I thought I needed to take. Unfortunately, my sense of direction was way off. I found a train, but it wasn't the one that would take me home.

The train I stood in front of was on lockdown. They were cleaning it, but I didn't know that. The last thing I remember thinking was, "Man, I need to get on this train, but I can't even think straight." Then I blacked out completely.

What must have been 40 minutes later, I woke up lying face down on the top of a train car catwalk. I looked to my left and to my right. I noticed the hair on my right arm was standing up like it was being affected by static electricity. I didn't think anything of it. I was way too disoriented and groggy to even begin to understand the situation I was in. It made no sense.

My only thought was, "What the hell am I doing on top of a train car?" All I wanted to do was get down and try to figure out what was actually going on. As I began to orient myself, I realized I was facing the end of the train car.

I could see steps that would lead me back to safety. It looked like it was going to be easy to get down. I looked to my right, and I saw a small rod I decided I was going to grab onto to stabilize myself as I shifted my body around to get onto the steps. My goal was just to get back to the train platform and get some help. I knew I needed it. Nothing made sense.

Without hesitation, I reached over and grabbed the rod. My life instantly changed forever as 13,800 volts of electricity pulsed through my body the moment my hand wrapped around the metal rod. My body caught on fire. My blood boiled at 985 degrees, and I screamed until I ran out of oxygen. And then I died.

Yes, I actually died, saw the "light" that many claim to see, and even was drawn to a beautiful gate (just like in the Bible). When I came back from death moments later, all I could think was, "I'm not going to let go yet! I'm going to fight for my life one more time!"

Shock Your Life Into Action

In the midst of pain most people will never experience in their lives, I chose to fight for my life. **I will never forget the decision I made to try to save myself when I could have let go.** This was just the beginning of a long road of transformation that would require more strength, courage, discipline and patience to carry out than I could have ever imagined. Whatever you are going through, you have a simple choice to make: should you let go? Or should you fight one more time? You owe it to yourself and your family to fight one more time.

"Should I let go? Or should I fight one more time?"

JESSE SINK

Chapter 4

The Gates of Heaven

When I died, I came out of my body. I floated above it, and I was able to look down at my searing flesh on top of the train. To my left, I saw two white doves and a bright, white light. Instinctively, I moved towards the light because it felt warm and peaceful.

As I got closer and closer to the light, all feelings of anger, anxiety or any type of negativity just melted away. The closer I got to the light, the more love and peace I experienced as it washed over my soul.

I experienced complete relief from all of the difficulties I'd ever experienced in life. There was nothing left to worry about. I didn't have to worry about my bills being paid, where my career was going or what anyone thought about me.

It's extremely difficult to describe the feelings of peace and wellness I felt. Think of the first time you ever fell in love, how euphoric you felt. That's how I felt multiplied by 10.

As I moved further into the light, a massive, golden gate appeared. As I got closer to it, the intensity of the light increased until it was all consuming. I got extremely close to the gate. It felt like I was going home, and I was just seconds from arrival. Then, all of the sudden, it was like a vacuum turned on, and I got sucked back down into my body.

I woke up from the dead. I gasped for air, and I realized I was breathing fire. Flames were all over my face. The clothes and backpack I was wearing were burning away, and plastic was melting down my back. This is when I realized I had a choice to make, and I chose to fight for my life.

My hand was still electrically drawn to the rod that had just sent 13,800 volts through my body. With the last bit of energy I had left, I used my free hand to pull my attached hand from the rod, and it released, sending my body hurtling face first into the concrete of the railway platform.

I remember my face smashing into the cold, hard concrete, but it felt like I had hit a foam pillow. It seemed soft and welcoming because nothing could compare to being lit on fire and melting from the inside out.

A guy cleaning the train heard what had happened. He saw me on fire on the ground, pulling melted plastic off of my back, moaning and screaming bloody murder. He quickly grabbed a fire extinguisher and sprayed me down. I remember he told me, "Don't move. I'm going to go get help. Stay where you are." Then he took off.

There was absolutely no way that I was just going to stay there. I was hurting so bad. The only thing I could do was try to escape the pain somehow. I started running as fast as I could to try to find more people to help me. There were no people on the platform I was on, so I jumped down and moved across two sets of tracks.

If I had stumbled across a track charged at 22,000 volts, my legs would have blown clear off. Somehow, I missed the tracks. As I came up to the platform where I could see there were people, I flopped my right hand on top of the walkway.

I tried to pull myself up, but my right arm would do nothing for me. It was just a black, charred, useless mess. But I couldn't focus on that. I needed to focus on finding help. I threw my left arm up onto the walkway, and using that side of my body I was able to hoist myself up.

As soon as people saw me clawing zombie-like out of the ditch, they screamed, and they ran the other way. I yelled to them, "I need help! Please, someone help me!" But this just caused them to run away even faster.

I can't blame them. I had melted plastic all over my upper body. My hair was burned. I had blood all over my face. I must've looked terrifying, like a demon crawling my way out of hell. If our roles were reversed, I probably would have turned the other way and ran as well.

I realized quickly that no one was going to help me, so I sat down against the wall. I tried to collect my thoughts and stay awake until the EMTs got there. I realized that was the best I could do.

As I sat there panting for breath, I leaned back against the wall. I tried to pull my backpack off, and my skin came with it. The raw meat of my body rubbed fresh blood up onto the wall, and I screamed in agony. I couldn't handle the pain of my skinless flesh touching anything, so I tried to stand up.

At that moment, a flood of people came barreling towards me. It seemed like it took them forever to get to me, even though I know they were moving as fast as possible. When they finally threw the gurney down, I remember the look in their eyes said it all. They could hardly believe I was still alive.

Shock Your Life Into Action

The serenity I experienced when I died for a moment is something I will never forget. It has totally changed the way I view life. I don't fully understand its significance, or why I had to leave that place, but the memory of it will always be with me. **Going from complete peace to total agony was the real shock of my life.**
Moments of peace are often followed by pain. And moments of pain are often followed by peace. It's part of the ride in life. No matter what you are going through (divorce, job loss, health issues, or depression), remember that it's all temporary. **Enjoy the ride. Be stronger than the obstacle that's in front of you.**

"Going from complete peace to total agony was the real shock of my life."

JESSE SINK

Chapter 5

Time Passed Without Me

I turned around backwards, and I body slammed myself onto the stretcher. I was in so much pain, I had no time to waste getting carefully onto it. I stared up at the EMTs, and they stared back. I said something to them like, "Buckle me up. Let's go."

They didn't say anything. They just strapped me up as best they could around my wounds. Blood was everywhere. I screamed again as they began to move me. The friction created between my skin-stripped, raw back and the stretcher felt like knives tearing through my skin.

I remember being loaded into the ambulance, and one of the EMTs had pulled my cell phone from my pocket. He scrolled through, called my dad and said, "Is your son Jesse Sink?" My dad confirmed I was his son, and then the EMT said, "He's in bad condition. He may only have a few days to live. We need you to come verify that this is your son."

I can only imagine what went through my dad's head at that time. I'm sure he was a mix of angry, scared and concerned. He had never approved of my lifestyle, and this probably looked like proof that he was right. But he scrambled to get everything in order at the farm, and he bought a ticket to New York.

The last thing I remember hearing on the ambulance was, "We have a patient with 60% burns to his upper body. We believe he might be homeless. Slight chance for survival."

I thought to myself, "Slight chance for survival? Dude, I'm here. I'm good. I'm breathing. Are you kidding me?" Then I blacked out.

At the hospital they had to give me 25% more drugs to keep me sedated than they give most people because my metabolism was so high. I spent 10 days in a coma, and after those 10 days I suddenly woke up. I looked up, and there was a light over my head. I was inside a surgery room.

Next, I felt a searing pain like someone had stuck a knife in my throat. Then I felt something pop into my throat. This was the doctors putting a trach in. After that, the light faded away, and I fell back into a coma for two months.

For two whole months, time passed without me. I only know of what happened during this time period from what my family has told me. I was fortunate to be under the care of some of the best burn doctors in the world. These were the same doctors who treated all of the 9/11 victims.

My dad showed up at the hospital a day after my accident. Everything about my physical appearance had been marred and disfigured by the flames. My dad accepted the fact that I was probably not going to live. He kissed me, and then he left the room crying. He identified me for the doctors. All he could do from there was hope and pray for the best. He has told me the only way he could recognize me was by my eyes.

When I finally opened them again, I saw a name taped to the light above my hospital bed. It was the name of my new nephew who had just recently been born. I saw this name, and then I saw my sister in the room. I didn't know what was going on at all, and then I fell back asleep.

These moments of wakefulness, followed by more sleep, happened because the doctors were pulling me out of the coma. This quick in and out went on for what must have been several hours at least until I finally woke up long enough to make eye contact with sister for a moment. She looked at me, and she said, "Hey, your eyes are open. Do you know what day it is today?"

I couldn't talk because I had the trach in my throat, but I shook my head "no." Then she said, "It's February 29th." At that moment, I heard my heart monitor start beeping very fast. I was totally confused.

I had no idea what had happened to me. I had no recollection of anything in that moment. I remember thinking, "Why is my sister in New York? Why is she in the hospital?" Nothing connected or made sense to me, and then I feel back asleep for I don't know how long.

When I woke up again, my sister told me, "You've been sleeping for two months. You got electrocuted." What she said still didn't connect, and I struggled to remain conscious long enough to make any sense of it. The truth is I wasn't ready to make sense of it for a long, long time.

Shock Your Life Into Action

Even when I was being taken to the hospital in the ambulance following my accident, I had no idea of the seriousness of the situation. I don't think the human mind can easily comprehend tragedy like I experienced, especially right in the middle of it. If I had understood anything other than the shear pain I was experiencing, I may have literally scared myself to death. I'm so thankful for the doctors and EMTs who did everything they could to save my life, even though it meant I had to disappear into a coma for two months.

There are going to be moments in life that you will feel completely asleep. You might even feel as if you are frozen in time. Sometimes there is nothing you can do about it. Think of it as a healing stage. Think of it as a period where your body, mind, and spirit are preparing you for the journey ahead. Then, when you **can do** something about it, it's time to do what you were born to do – MAKE UP FOR LOST TIME.

"They won't even let me die. They want me here."

JESSE SINK

Chapter 6

The Second Shock

As I continued to fade in and out of consciousnesses, I slowly tried to gain controlled movement of my body. I didn't have the strength to move my head from side to side or keep my neck straight. They'd given me drugs to induce the coma, and they had to give me different drugs to bring me out of it slowly.

As they brought me back out, I went through what someone experiences when they're going through heroin withdrawals. I experienced nightmares, cold sweats, tremors and vomiting. It was horrifying.

When I finally got my wits about me, I felt something weird on my right hand. It felt like there was a glove on it. I peeked down to see what was going on, and I saw that my arm from the elbow down was completely gone. It had been hacked off, the end covered with massive white bandages.

I quickly glanced at the rest of my body, and I saw I had horrible scars all over my stomach. I didn't know what was going on, and I couldn't figure it out. At that moment, I panicked. My heart rate went through the roof. The heart monitor I was hooked up to started beeping wildly.

I had a panic attack from the shock I experienced trying to make sense of what I just saw—my body completely destroyed. They had to come in and give me a shot of something to calm me down. After the shot, I sunk back into the darkness.

I'd been laying in a coma so long my muscles had deteriorated. In two months, I went from 200 pounds to 143 pounds. I couldn't even feed myself. My dad had to spoon-feed me. I couldn't even hold a piece of popcorn in my palm. It took three days for me to come completely out of the coma. As I gained more and more consciousnesses, I kept thinking to myself, "Man, I need to call my agent. I don't know what's going on, but I need to tell him I'm hurt." However, I couldn't talk. It felt like I had a bunch of gunk stuck in my throat.

Eventually, I got the strength to look over to my mom who was sitting in my hospital room, and I mouthed to her, "Why did they cut my arm off?"

She just started shaking and crying. She grabbed my arm, and she said, "Jesse, they had to." She continued to tell me through tears, "It turned gangrene, and it had to be taken off 10 days in. I'm so sorry."

At this point, I still didn't comprehend what had happened to me. I mouthed to my mom, "What's going on? Why am I here?" And she told me what happened, how I had been at the train station, gotten on top of a train car and grabbed onto a hot wire that burned my whole upper body.

It didn't make sense to me. I tried to absorb it, but I couldn't do it. I had another panic attack. Then I started bawling. In my mind, I told myself, "Well, I'm just going to quit breathing. This is stupid. I have to be dreaming. If I stop breathing, I'll either wake up, or I'll die. If this is for real, then I don't want to be alive."

So I quit breathing. But it didn't work. I was on a ventilator, so when I stopped breathing, the ventilator worked against me and forced me to breathe again.

When I stopped breathing, my lips would turn blue. This was the cue for the nurse to shove a tack through my toenail and into my toe to make me gasp for air. It hurt so bad, and it pissed me off. I kept thinking, "Do you not see me here? I'm trying to get rid of myself because I'm miserable!"

But each time I would try to stop breathing, the nurse would do this. I was so angry about it that I kept trying to smash her hand against the end of the bed to make her stop saving me.

One time, I missed hitting the nurse's hand, and I hit the end of the bed full force. I almost broke the end of the bed off. My mom yelled at me louder than I'd ever heard her yell before, "Jesse! Stop!" I remember the nurse chiming in, "Man, that was close. Stop, Jesse. Breathe." (I included a picture of this amazing person in the photo gallery.)

I was angry, and I thought to myself, "They won't even let me die. They want me here." At that point, I gave up. I quit fighting against my breath, and I let the ventilator do the work. I had no choice but to go on living, even though it was the last thing I wanted to do.

Shock Your Life Into Action

My mind for many reasons did not let me accept what had happened to me right away. When it finally sunk in, I no longer wanted to live. I did everything I could to make myself die, but it was clear that I could not escape through death. **Every time I tried to, the people around me fought to bring me back.** I had no choice but to accept what had happened and face an extremely uncertain future. Even when I did begin to grasp the concept of what had happened to me, it didn't feel real. There are people around you fighting for you to live. You might not see it or feel it, but they are there. Even if you want to die inside, there are so many people who want you to live. Live for them. In the end, it's the best way to say "thank you."

"I took a different road than my father through life, so help me God. All things are possible."

JESSE SINK

Chapter 7

Fighting Back

A week passed before I was able to move my body around enough to get in and out of a chair. All the drugs pumped through my system made it difficult for me to even see straight. My whole body was filled with toxic chemicals designed to keep me sedated.

I hadn't yet seen what my whole body looked like. But one of the nurses asked me, "Jesse, would you like to see if we can stand you up in a walker, go over to the mirror and let you have a look at you?"

I said, "Yeah, sure. Let's try it." When they stood me up, I felt awful. But I hobbled over in front of the mirror, and the nurses held me up in front of it.

One of them told me, "I just want you to see yourself so you can see who you are now." I knew who Jesse was before the accident, but there was no way I could have prepared for what I saw in the mirror. I didn't recognize myself at all.

All I could recognize was my blue eyes, the same eyes my dad recognized when he had to identify my body the day after my accident. At that moment, I started crying and shaking, and the nurses took me back to my hospital bed.

I lay down, and I thought to myself, "I have no idea if I'll ever look like I used to." I had no idea what was happening. I didn't even know if what I was experiencing was truly real or not. I decided I was just going to let myself fall asleep, take a nap and hope and pray that when I woke up again, it would all turn out to be a stupid, sick dream.

I woke up about two hours later, and I pinched myself on my leg. In that moment, I had to accept I was not in a dream. It was all real, and there was no way around it. There was no way to escape my reality. I couldn't go back and change what had happened to me.

I had to accept my new reality, my new body, whether I wanted to or not. I didn't know how to deal with it. There was no real way for me to deal with it. All I could do was what everyone kept telling me to do—just breathe.

That's all I did for the next couple of days until I got the strength to sit up on my own. Several weeks later, they unhooked me from the IV drips, and they took me out of the ICU. I began to breathe on my own, but my breathing was irregular, in and out. For two months, I'd been breathing with the help of a machine. My body didn't know how to do it on its own anymore. I had to relearn how to do it.

    I no longer knew how to walk. I needed help to take a shower. It was like I had been reduced to living the life of a child. I was completely dependent on everyone else around me to take care of me. My mind was hazy, but it was still my mind. This might sound like a good thing, but it was torturous. I was now a soul trapped inside of a body I could no longer control.

    I endured many sleepless nights in my bed at the New York Presbyterian Hospital. I stared at the bridge lights outside of my window and cried until I was finally exhausted enough to fall asleep.

    The painkillers I was on stopped working. I became immune to them. The pain I was in hit me all over and caused me to toss and turn in my bed. There was nothing I could do to escape the pain except for fall asleep. I tried to commit suicide in the bed, but I lived.

    My mom and dad were there with me the whole the time. My distant family traveled to come see me. And, eventually, the day came when we all had to face the question, "What's going to happen with Jesse?"

    A psychiatrist came with his assistant to talk with me. The first thing they asked me was, "Why were you doing coke on top of the train?"

I looked at them, and I said, "Doing coke? What are you talking about? I don't even know how I got on top of the train." Then the psychiatrist told me they had found coke in my bloodstream.

I was angry about this. I felt like I was being blamed for what had happened to me, but I hadn't been doing coke that night. What they had found was a little bit of coke in my bloodstream from two days earlier. They hadn't tested for the roofie I suspected somebody had placed in my drink that night. All they had done was look at their basic drug screen result, and then they started putting a story together that was just plain wrong.

I told the psychiatrist, "Look, I'm a fitness model. I'm not a drug addict. I don't know what happened, but you've got the story wrong." They kept asking me questions until I exploded in rage. I yelled at them to get out of my room. I was ready to physically beat them out of my room with all the strength I could muster.

Then my mom walked in, and she told them, "You better leave. This is not going to end well." When they were gone, I screamed at my mom, "Do not let those two back into this room ever again! I never want to see them again in my life. I'm not going to be ridiculed with false information!" The false story was dropped, never to be brought up again.

Shock Your Life Into Action

The pain I experienced as I really gained consciousness of my situation was devastating. In spite of that, I was fortunate to be surrounded by people who loved me. When the hospital tried to put together my story the wrong way, I fought against being labeled as a reckless drug addict. That was not who I was, and I refused to accept that story. I fought for my dignity, just like I've had to many times since.

Sometimes, people will figure you all wrong in life. Many people will assume the worst about you and others will judge you immediately. It's your job to set the record straight and let people know the real story. **Fight for the truth.** After all, that's what people will remember the most about you.

"God, I believe you kept me here for a reason. Prove that to me. I will wait until you do."

JESSE SINK

Chapter 8

Help on the Road to Recovery

When I began rehab, I was an inner tube of scar tissue. The rehab facilitators began by stretching and tearing the tissue in my body to make it longer. This is a painful process. I also had to learn to walk again because my whole body was stiff. I couldn't move without experiencing pain.

When you've been lying down for two months, walking again is tough. Your knees ache. Everything about the movement is exhausting. On top of that, my will to do all the work was not very strong. I didn't understand why I'd lived at all, but I kept moving forward.

I had extreme PTSD from the accident. I was taking a huge amount of painkillers and Oxycontin to keep myself stable. For the first four months of my recovery, I lived with my parents. But after a while, I felt very isolated. They lived in Tukwila, Washington, in the middle of nowhere, and it was freezing cold and snowy while I was there.

I got very depressed because I felt stuck. I'd tried so hard to get away from my parents' home when I was younger, and there I was back living with them again. I told my mom how thankful I was for their help, and that I loved them. But I also told her I needed to leave, which was hard. I didn't want to make my parents upset, but I was so unhappy I would have rather been dead. I needed to be around people again. I couldn't keep hiding away from the world.

Eventually, we worked out arrangements for me to move in with my sister and her husband. Once I started living with them, things began to improve little by little. Mentally, I was still depressed. But I got a job at a steel trailer factory doing paperwork and answering phones just to make some money. It was better than sitting at home and doing nothing.

I had no idea what the next blueprint for my life was going to look like. I had worked on my body for so many years. I had thought modeling was going to be my path. Now everything I had worked for was burned and gone, and I had to start completely over. I had no clue how to do that, but life kept barreling on and pushing me forward.

When I moved in with my sister, I started hanging out with people from the church we went to, the same kind of church we went to growing up. They were loving and helpful. They prayed for me. They fought for my wellbeing.

Even though they didn't understand my life and the choices I had made, they cared about me anyway. That was amazing to me. I learned from them that it doesn't matter if you understand someone's struggle or not. What matters is that you love them anyway.

After I had lived with my sister for about eight months, I got the courage to move again, and I moved in with my brother. This is when I started to get my feet underneath me again. I got my driver's license, paid off some bills and bought an older car so I could get from point A to point B on my own. I also bought a brand new laptop, which was the first computer I'd ever owned.

All this stuff might seem small, but it gave me some hope. I started to think, "Well, maybe all I've got is an old car, a laptop, some clothes and a meal on the table, but this could be my new blueprint." I started to feel like I was coming out of something, like I had survived something I wasn't supposed to survive. And for a reason. It was a small spark, but it was enough to renew some of my hope for the future. I kept praying, "God, I believe you kept me here for a reason. Prove that to me. I will wait until you do."

I started to gain small pieces of myself back little by little, and then I got a side gig helping some females do runway modeling. All the time I was thinking, "I should be dead, man." But the fact that I had lived spurred me forward, and I began to realize I had something. I had my story, and the simple fact that I was alive was enough to prove the rest of my life had a bigger purpose.

    I hoped I could maybe inspire some people to do the things that didn't work out for me. I didn't have any clear indication of how I could do that, but the wheels started turning. I was back on the road.

Shock Your Life Into Action

Under my family's care, I began to gain some hope for my future. It was the little things that inspired me to try to create a new life and follow a new blueprint. I didn't know how I was going to do it, but I was open to trying. Being open to the possibilities was the seed I needed to plant in order to start living life again. I had to believe I was here for a reason, because there was no other explanation for why I survived. When the "old" you is becoming the "new" you, you need a new **blueprint** to follow. Life changes people. Whether you experience change financially, spiritually, mentally, or physically, when you do, a new blueprint of your future must be created by you (and you alone). If you are ready to transform your surroundings, you must first start where all engineers start—at the drawing board. Creating the new you shouldn't be looked at as a bad thing. It should be looked at as simply the beginning of a new chapter. Even if it feels scary, it can be the most **freeing experience**. Trust me.

It's time to be done with this part of your life. It's time for you to move on."

JESSE SINK

Chapter 9

Nothing to Lose

With hope in my chest, I walked into Macy's. I had a job interview to work there, but I wasn't really dressed for the occasion. I did the best I could with some old pants and a nice button up shirt, but at the time I didn't think my strength was in my appearance. All I had was my story and the desire to improve my life in any small way that I could.

I remember talking to a friend before the interview, and I told him, "Dude, I'm so frustrated. I haven't had a job in a long time. But I've got nothing to lose. I'm just going to tell this guy at Macy's my story, tell him how I used to model, and see if I can get hired to work in the fashion part of Macy's."

When I finished telling my story to the manager interviewing me at Macy's, he said to me, "That's amazing. Hearing you tell that story gave me a piece of hope. It's incredible what you went through, and you still look great. You're a good looking guy."

It made me feel great to know I inspired someone, and I appreciated the compliment on my appearance. A few days later, I got a call, and I was offered the job. The manager told me on my first day that he thought I was lying when I told him my story, so he went and Googled me. He couldn't believe I was standing in front of him ready to start putting my life back together in any way I could.

It was a huge relief for me to finally have a job where I got to interact with the public. It was nerve racking at first. I wasn't sure how people were going to react to me. But I went out, and I bought a suit to wear to the job, and I cleaned myself up a little bit. I tanned a little, and I did my hair.

My first day on the floor, two beautiful females walked up to me, and they said to each other, "He's really handsome." And I thought to myself, "Thank you, God, for giving me a little bit of light." After I worked there for a while, I started working as what they called a fragrance model. What I did was stand out in front of the fragrance counter, and I represented a couple of different colognes. I began to feel the light coming back into my life. I was doing a form of modeling, and I felt very grateful.

But as time went on, I started to become jaded and angry. It was now three years after my accident, and I was still walking around without a right arm. I started drinking and partying more because I felt stuck again.

THE SHOCK OF A LIFETIME

I wasn't making much money. I wasn't progressing in my life, and I felt like I couldn't grow. I started working at a restaurant next door to Macy's as a host, just to pay my bills, and I tried to keep my head strong. I reminded myself that I was going through a transition, and I believed at the end of the journey would be something worth all of the effort. But it was a long, slow climb with many setbacks.

I had self-esteem issues. I didn't like my scars. I didn't enjoy myself, and I wasn't lifting or taking care of myself very well. In fact, to deal with all the confusion that was going on in my head, I did whatever I could to escape and numb the pain. I had to do something to pass the time, so I drank with friends. I was young and searching for a footing somewhere, so I started partying a lot.

I came out of my partying phase with two DUIs, 30 days in jail and 30 days at an inpatient treatment center. I could have been given a year of jail time for the DUIs. I believe the judge had sympathy for me in my situation, and I thank God for that. I wish I had chosen to take a smarter path, but I know looking back that I was doing the best that I could.

Going to the inpatient treatment center was the best thing that could have happened to me. I felt like it was God saying to me, "Hey, Jesse, look—it's time to be done with this part of your life. It's time for you to move on." I was not an alcoholic. I was just having fun with my friends, but I saw where more involvement with alcohol could lead.

I knew alcohol wasn't the answer to my problems all along, but this crystallized that truth for me. When I got out of the treatment center, I told myself I would never, ever let myself fall back into that situation again.

But the battle for my independence was just beginning. Following my inpatient treatment, I was sent back home to live with my parents for 90 days of house arrest. It was like I was starting all over again, but this time with an ankle bracelet hidden under my pants while I sat in church with my parents on Sunday mornings, just like I'd done as a child.

Shock Your Life Into Action

When I got the job at Macy's, it was the beginning of getting my life moving in the right direction. But I still had a lot of internal work to do. I had hope, but I was still searching for the meaning in my experience. I was still angry and frustrated that I had to start from the bottom again, and I didn't like myself. My stay in the inpatient treatment center, and the 90-days I spent on house arrest at my parents were the final push I needed. I became determined to claw my way back to the happy, successful and inspiring life I had always wanted to live.

There is always hope right around the corner. All you have to do is play the game of life with a **nothing to lose** mentality. It's amazing how many great people are out there willing to give you a chance if you give them a chance. Momentum can be found in the strangest of places,

"...I had become a force to be reckoned."

JESSE SINK

Chapter 10

A Force to Be Reckoned With

When I finally took my ankle bracelet off after 90 days of house arrest, I looked at my mom, and I said, "I'm so glad that happened. It sucked, but I needed this to ground myself and figure out what I want in life."

I had spent those three months of house arrest looking at myself in the mirror. It was difficult to once again be back in my parents' home, but at this time they were living in Chewelah, Washington, surrounded by mountains and nature. I had no choice but to become very introspective in that setting.

When I came out of it, I realized that whether I liked it or not, it was exactly what I needed to shape me. Living there was exactly what I needed to get everything back on track, but there was still a long, uphill climb ahead. I had $30,000 of debt I needed to pay off from all the costs associated with the DUIs. I had to get serious about making things right. I had a massive amount of work to do.

The first thing I did was I bought a car (with the help of a friend who co-signed the loan), and I took on four jobs. I met a lady who had lost her husband from cancer. We worked on her new house that she was building. I did everything. Painting, building wood tables and doing whatever I could possible do to help her. She helped me raise around $10,000 for my arm and pay off many bills. **Thank you Julie Luke and Steven Bauman!** One of the jobs was weeding grass and pulling leaves out of gravel landscaping. I got down on my knees, and pulled weeds with one hand. I did it until my knees bled. I didn't care what it was going to take to get my life back in order. **I was determined to do it.**

I cried sometimes when I was out pulling weeds, because I was so fed up and tired with my joints aching, and head pounding from the heat of the sun. In one instance, I was pulling weeds in some guy's garden, and he came out with a whole cup full of Captain Morgan. He looked at me working, and he said, "I don't know who you are, or where you came from, but do you want this?"

I started laughing, and I looked up at him and said, "You know, I might have a sip." I took one sip, and I immediately thought to myself, "What are you doing, Jesse?

Look at where this got you." The next thing I did was dump the entire cup out on the ground, and I kept working. I was frustrated with the situation I had gotten myself into, and there was no way I was going to make the same mistake more than once.

I took any kind of work I could get during this time. If I could fit it into my schedule, I did it. It didn't matter what it was. I had a friend who understood my situation, and he helped me find different odd jobs I could go do.

After a year of working non-stop, I was almost debt free. I decided it was time to make a huge change. I decided I was going to move to LA to see what I could do in the entertainment business. I'd had enough of my low self-esteem. I'd had enough of working myself into the dirt.

So many people had judged me at that point, I felt like no one could hold me back. Nothing anyone could say to me could hurt me in any way. I was ready to show myself to the world, scars and all. I didn't want to bury them anymore in any way.

I knew that if I was put in front of a camera, I was going to be real. I wasn't going to hold anything back. So I moved to Los Angeles, California, and I started working as a fitness trainer.

While working as a trainer, I ended up running into a lady who did public relations work. I started working with her, and that was the first time I ever told my full story to somebody. She was completely blown away by what I told her. And she said to me, "Wow, we've got to do something big with this."

This was the first time I was able to look at my story and really see how powerful it was. My family was certainly not impressed by it, and up to that point, I didn't know how the public would respond to it, either.

But I realized that the fact that I was still alive meant that I needed to share all that I've gone through. With even more fire in my belly, I started training even harder in the gym to keep strengthening and improving my body. Not only that, I entered a life coaching program.

I knew I needed to invest in my mind as well as body. I needed to dump the baggage I was carrying around with me, and I needed to start fresh. I learned so much through life coaching about myself and about other people, and it really helped me get my mind right.

As the pieces started to come together for me in LA, I became even more determined to succeed. I began to see that through the accident and my slow and painful recovery, I had become a force to be reckoned. And as long as I can still breathe, I'm going to continue to fight for the life I want to live.

Shock Your Life Into Action

I had to pay for mistakes, and I paid for them big time. But I did my time, and I moved on. I wasn't going to let anything in my past hold me back from going after the life I wanted for myself. When I finally got the chance to tell my story to someone in LA, that's when I realized how powerful it was. I became even more determined to move forward towards my goals, and I decided I would never let anything hold me back. There is so much power in your backstory. No matter what you have been through, it can and should be used to help others in their own lives. **Strength comes from muscle breakdown.** For that reason, every time you come across a period of struggle, understand that it is actually making you stronger. Enough struggle will cause you to become **a force to be reckoned with.**

"Don't take yourself so seriously."

JESSE SINK

Chapter 11

Go All the Way

When I started making contacts with people out in LA that saw something special in my story, that's when things started to click for me. I thought, "Hell, I should make a movie out of all these crazy experiences I've had."

I kept working hard in the gym. People started to know who I was, and eventually I met a writer who had a reputation for directing biography films and helping people to sell their story. It felt like fate. I was so thankful that the things I'd always wanted to be a part of my life were now appearing.

When I lived with my family for all those years following my accident, I always felt that although they loved me, they thought I was a screw up. Since my family is so conservative, the choice I made to leave and pursue something else in my life that was outside of their comfort zone made me the black sheep. They accepted me, and I'm thankful they supported me in my recovery.

But even through all my pain and struggle, I held on tight to the idea that I was meant to do something more than just stay on the farm. Don't get me wrong. I loved my childhood. I had a lot of fun on the farm as a kid.

I was a very happy, carefree kid. I used to run and hop on the backs of pigs. Pigs can run extremely fast and reach top speed within just a few strides. Riding them around in my childhood was like riding little miniature horses, a huge rush.

On top of that, I spent many days just wandering around the farm playing with the cats, chasing chickens, riding my bike and running barefoot in the dirt. It was a simple life, and I wouldn't change it for the world.

However, as I got older, life pulled me in a different direction. I don't believe we're meant to stay in one place forever. When we try to do that, we end up being miserable and depressed. We're ordained to grow.

In LA, when I began to see that people believed in the power of my story, my personal growth exploded. For the first time in my life, I felt accepted for exactly who I always believed I was. Having people around me that believed in me inspired me to go all the way.

So I took my story, and I advertised it, and I got some film work. I started doing movies, and I got myself more acquainted with the industry. Then I worked on a screenplay with the help of some incredible individuals, and that's currently, at the time of this writing, being shopped around in Hollywood.

As the pieces began to fall into place, I put my head down, and I kept on working hard. I trained to the point where I got my body to look even better than it did before my accident. This fact alone blew me away. The fact that I could come from not even wanting to be alive to now feeling and looking better than ever before made me extremely grateful. I still live life from this place of gratitude today.

With my newfound confidence, I decided to enter a men's physique contest. This was huge for me because it meant that I had just gone from wanting to hide the scars on my body a couple years prior, to wanting to display my body on stage for everyone to see. When I got on stage, I saw people watching me with tears in their eyes because they were so inspired by me and what I had gone through to rebuild my body from the ground up.

The videographer at the event came up to me afterwards, and she was shaking with emotion as she talked to me. She told me, "I don't know what you're doing, but keep doing it." This was another moment of light for me, a confirmation that I was on the right path.

I ended up winning the men's physique contest, and I got fifth place in both categories I entered. Winning was an incredible feeling, but things got even better from there.

Immediately following the contest, I was offered a sponsorship by a major sports nutrition company.

It was like a dream come true. I became a sponsored athlete. I went home that night, and I looked in the mirror. All I could do was look at myself and cry. I felt in my heart in that moment that one day I would be able to say I was actually glad I'd had the accident that burned me alive.

I still had pain. I still thought to myself, "What if? What if this had never happened to me?" But the joy I felt in that moment overpowered that question, and I put it out of my mind. Instead of thinking about the "what ifs," I said to myself, "I believe a time is going to come where something wonderful beyond my wildest imagination is going to happen to me, and I'm going to keep fighting and going all in until it does."

Shock Your Life Into Action

I've had the support of so many incredible people on my journey. But by far the most important part of my ability to bounce back after my accident has been my unwillingness to ever give up on myself. I've had to decide over and over that no matter what happens to me, I'm going to fight for my life. I will never back down, and I will never quit. It's either all or nothing for me. I've made up my mind that I'm going to go all the way, or I'm going to die trying.

Are you ready to go all the way for what you want? If not, you are simply giving up on yourself. Don't you dare give up on yourself.

Think positive, creative thoughts, and guard your mind from negativity."

JESSE SINK

Chapter 12

I'm Not Them

When I moved to LA, my family was terrified. Rightly so, because the last time I moved somewhere, I died. But I knew God had bigger plans for me than to continue to play it safe and live an average life. Although my family questioned me, I didn't doubt I had made the right choice to move away.

So when I got the athletic sponsorship, I buckled up, put my helmet on, and said, "Let's roll." I ran with it. I made it my purpose to inspire the people around me to be better, to work even harder in spite of all the odds. At every event I went to as an athlete, people would come up to me, shake my hand and tell me how much I had inspired them.

I learned a lot about the fitness industry and myself throughout this time. I learned there are a lot of egocentric people involved in it, which makes sense—bodybuilding is all about displaying yourself. It's a very "puff out your chest" type of industry.

But that wasn't my approach to it. I had never lifted weights in order to show off for other people. I always did it because it was therapeutic for me, and I wanted to take care of myself. Any recognition I got for the body I built in the process was just a bonus.

My approach to entering the professional the men's physique world was much different than everybody else's approach. I thought to myself, "You know what? I could be the one dude in this industry to come in and disarm everyone. I could show people what this industry should really be about. It could use a dose of humility."

I took this on as my purpose, and soon I signed a deal for an even better sponsorship. The company I signed with wanted to move me up in their ranks and have me do different stuff to promote their brand, but they weren't offering to pay me anything more than the original agreement.

Right away, I felt like something was off. I felt like they wanted to use me to make themselves look good, but they weren't willing to offer me any financial help in return. I didn't want to just become a spokesperson for a brand that didn't put their money where their mouth was.

I had people coming up to me at shows telling me, "Dude, you're the most inspiring person in your whole company that I know of. Why aren't you featured on their displays?" I was relatively new at the time, and I didn't have a good answer to that question.

I went to the guy in charge of the company and asked him, and he couldn't give me a good answer other than that featuring me was going to cost the company too much money. I didn't feel supported or cared about, so I left the company. I signed out of my contract, and they were shocked. But I couldn't stand being a part of a company that didn't believe in me at the time. I'd dealt with too much of that in my life already. I wanted to work with people who believed in me as much as I believed in myself. There was no other way around it. I had to quit on the spot.

Making the decision to end my contract caused me to struggle financially. Even though I knew it was the right decision to make, I didn't know what was going to happen next. But I did what I had to do because I had faith that things were going to turn out all right. I'd already cheated death in my life, what could possibly be more difficult to do than that?

I kept lifting hard and doing bodybuilding. I worked so hard and so intensely that I kept breaking my prosthetic arms. Every two or three months, my arm would break.

After I broke several arms, the doctor started to question me. He asked me, "What are you doing? How do you keep breaking these?" Then I showed him the videos of me bench pressing 455 pounds with a prosthetic arm. He couldn't believe it. He told me, "People with two arms can't even do this."

All I could say back was, "I'm not them." The doctor wanted me to slow down, but I couldn't accept that. All of my life I had been told I needed to do that, and I knew that to slow down would mean I would have to go against my very nature. All my life I had been treated like a tiger in a cage, and there was no way I was going to go back in the cage willingly. No way.

I told my doctor, "I don't know what limits are. I'm never going to accept limits. If I accept limits, then I will be tying myself up. I'm disgusted with myself that I used to do less with two hands than I do now with one."

Through this conversation, I came to the full realization that I had totally transformed my thinking and myself. I was no longer in any way a victim of a tragic accident. I was a phoenix that had risen out of the ashes, and I was going to keep flying as high as I could reach—no matter what.

Shock Your Life Into Action

Never accept limits other people try to put on you. There are no limits in life. You are only limited by what you believe you can do. If you believe you can do the impossible, you will do it. My struggle has taught me that I can never accept being a victim. If you have life, you have opportunity. Run with that opportunity. Don't let anybody tell you what you can or can't do. **Rise out of the ashes, and fly as high as you can—no matter what.**

"I used the only tools I had available to me. It felt like a shot in the dark, but I had nothing to lose."

JESSE SINK

Chapter 13

Don't Settle for "No"

My prosthetic arms continued to break because of the stress I put them under doing hardcore weightlifting. My co-payment to get these arms replaced was about $3,000 every single time I broke one. It got to be very expensive because I was breaking them every couple of months. It started to hurt me a lot financially. So much so that I set up a GoFundMe for people to help me out with the payments. I didn't know what else to do. I couldn't give up what I loved to do.

Around this same time, I lost my car. I got rear-ended, and it totaled my car. This was the car I bought back when I was doing my time, working incredibly hard to pay off all the money I owed from the DUIs I had. It was completely paid off, but I was left with nothing after the accident. I had to start paying to Uber around everywhere in LA, which got to be very expensive.

On top of this, I lost my insurance, and then my prosthetic arm broke again. For six months, I didn't know what to do with myself. I just sat at home, and I became depressed. I couldn't even work out.

I felt like I was losing the traction I had worked so hard to build up. I was back down to zero. I started to question myself again. I wondered if I had made the right decision to dump my athletic sponsorship contract.

It tore me up inside, but I realized I couldn't dwell on that. I made the choice to move on from that contract because I valued myself, and I knew there had to be something better for me out there in the world. There was no way I was going to stop valuing myself and respecting the decisions I had made in the past just because things were not looking good for me.

But I knew if there was one thing I'd learned from all of my experiences, it was that I could not allow myself to give up. It didn't matter how many times life knocked me down, I was determined to stand back up again and fight.

I took a long, hard look at myself, and I told myself, "You're not going to settle, punk." I stood up, and I kept going. I was not going to settle for "no." I decided that I had nothing to lose. I decided I was going to go in to my insurance company and be real. I was going to go talk to them face to face, and I was going to throw my heart out on the table. They could judge me all they wanted to, because I didn't care at that point.

So I walked into my insurance company's office, and I told them, "You're going to give me my insurance back." They tried to tell me that because of what I was doing with my prosthetic arm, I wasn't disabled. They had no idea that I wasn't about to give up that easily. I demanded that they fix the situation and give me my insurance back, or I was going to take legal action against them.

They had put me down as "not disabled" to get out of having to cover the costs of paying for my broken prosthetics, but my situation hadn't changed. Just because I was bodybuilding and working towards improving myself, that did not mean I had magically grown my arm back. I told the guy at the company, "If my arm grows back, I'll let you know. But until then, I'm disabled. So let's get my insurance back."

That very moment, the guy I was talking to went and got his manager, and they gave me my insurance back on the spot. Usually, this process would have taken six months, but they overrode the whole process. They sent me out my insurance check the very next month, and I got my arm back, as well as my dignity.

I started working out again and doing private training, but my financial situation was still not good. My arm continued to break every couple of months, and the co-payments started to drag me under again. I had to do anything I could to make money, so I sold some of the supplements I had left over from my sponsorship for enough cash to keep me afloat just a little bit longer.

I didn't know how I was going to make it out of this situation, but I thought if I could get some kind of sponsorship for my prosthetic arm, it would help me out immensely. I knew to get that sort of sponsorship, I was going to have to get serious about my purpose. I was going to have to get back to working hard to inspire other people also going through tough times to keep fighting. I was going to have to dig deep to keep myself going and continue to share my story with the world.

I used the only tools I had available to me to do that. It felt like a shot in the dark, but I had nothing to lose. I used social media, the videos of me doing things people believed were impossible for me, and my story of how even when it feels like life is pitting everything against you, you can never settle for "no."

Shock Your Life Into Action

Life has knocked me down more times than I can count, but I've always stood up and refused to take "no" for an answer. There's nothing that life can throw at you that you can't handle. Where there's a will, there's a way. Use what you have available to you to dig yourself out of the hole if you fall into one. **Don't fear other people judging you. They're not the ones living your life. Be real. Put your heart on the table, and take back your dignity.**

"You can create magic out of pain."

JESSE SINK

Chapter 14

Magic Out of Pain

I envisioned a sponsorship for my prosthetic arm to end the financial trouble it kept causing me, and I went after it in the best way I knew how. Through my use of social media and networking with people whenever I could, I met a woman who helped me get on a national TV show called The Doctors.

This was a huge break for me. It blew my mind that people cared about my story enough for it to be featured on national TV. Right before I went on the show to be filmed, I could hardly breathe. I was shaking because I was so uncomfortable.

I felt exactly how I felt when I did my first runway show in New York. I was a bundle of nerves. I was nervous about sharing my story with such a huge audience. Before I went on the show, I prayed, "God, give me strength. Help me stay calm. Whatever I need to speak to the world, let me speak it."

I told myself, "Once you sit down, you're going to be good. Don't worry." Then I headed out onto the stage. As soon as I sat down, one of the doctors on the show looked at me and said, "What you've done is amazing. I've never seen anyone come back from something like you went through. Your story inspires so many people."

The Doctors TV show ended up buying me a new prosthetic arm, and it's the one I still wear to this day. This was a huge answer to prayer. They told me after the show that I had made it one of the best shows they'd done in a long time. I didn't do anything special when I was on the show besides share my story in the same way I've shared it with you in this book.

In the audience, people were crying. They couldn't believe what I had gone through. It was very moving for me to be on such a big stage sharing the story of my transformation. It put pressure on me to do even better in life, and to make even better decisions because I wanted to be able to show everyone what is possible if they never give up on themselves.

After my appearance on the TV show, I started to make some different decisions. I stopped hanging around with certain people I knew weren't a good influence on me. I kept to myself. I stayed home quite a bit. Financially, I was not better off than before I went on the show.

In fact, things got even tougher for me. I was still training people, but the money was just not coming in fast enough. It got so bad that I had to go get food stamps so I could eat. I didn't even have enough money to buy basic food for myself after my rent was paid, and I felt so stupid.

I cried on my way to get the food stamps because I felt like a failure. But I told myself, "Jesse, it's okay. You need some help right now, and that doesn't make you any weaker. It doesn't make you a failure. You will rise above this, just like you've risen above all the other obstacles in your life."

I was at another low point, but I was still processing some of the things I had learned when I went through life coaching. The most important thing I learned is that what you think, you create. I realized I needed to work as hard on improving my thoughts and making them more positive as I had always worked on my body.

This became my focus. I didn't want to be a victim of negative thoughts. I wanted to be the hero of my story. So I started thinking of ways that I could turn my financial situation around I started thinking positively about my business, because I wanted to start attracting higher quality clients. I wanted to get clients that would pay me more money to work with them than I was used to getting, so I started focusing my mind on this result.

What came to me through my intuition was that people wanted to work with me as a trainer because I understood all the obstacles they were facing in their lives. It wasn't just what I knew about the physical body that was my strength. It was the fact that I was willing to listen to my clients' real life problems. That is what has made me the standout, sought after trainer I am today.

When I started to realize that my work was all about supporting other people in any way I could, that's when my private training business went through the roof. Instead of servicing a large number of clients for a low price, I concentrated on servicing a select few clients to the best of my ability, and I started charging them what I believed I was actually worth. This made all the difference for me, and it's a big reason why I'm now financially stable.

I realized my story is important because it allows me to connect with other people. But the really important work I do is possible because of who I've become as the result of all I've endured in my life. I understand what it means to struggle, and I don't judge anyone for the position they are currently in. I see people for who they when they come to me for help, but I also see who they can become if they work hard enough.

THE SHOCK OF A LIFETIME

I've learned that strength is a state of mind. What you think holds you back can actually move you forward. You can create magic out of pain.

Shock Your Life Into Action

Being on national TV showed me that people are watching. After that, I chose to make even better decisions, and I decided I needed to surround myself with the right people to support me in that goal. I struggled financially, but I began to focus even more on my mind. I realized that thoughts become things, and I began to think even more positively about my future. When I did that, my financial situation started to change, I was able to help more people, and I created magic out of my pain. **You can do the same.**

"Setbacks are temporary. Don't let them define you."

JESSE SINK

Chapter 15

Setbacks are Temporary

Back when I was "doing my time," working four jobs and living with family, I had a major realization that's stuck with me ever since. On top of doing all the work I was doing, I was also training my body in the gym.

I got my diet on point. I started working out and pushing myself, and I noticed that my body was responding positively. It didn't seem like this should be possible. After all, I wasn't even supposed to survive my accident. But there I was, regenerating my body little by little.

It blew me away that my body could go through what it went through and still perform at such a high level. So I entered a powerlifting competition in order to really test myself.

THE SHOCK OF A LIFETIME

On the day of the competition, I completed a 624 pound squat with one arm. I needed some assistance getting it 100% up, but in my mind, I had done it. This was the equivalent of breaking a USA record. I had done it before not in competition, and that was enough for me.

There were 40 people watching me as I did this squat. Not one of them walked away without being inspired to work harder in their lives. More importantly, they saw that it doesn't matter how much life beats you up, you can always make a comeback. There's always a second chance to get back out there and strive for greatness.

I don't know what inspired you to pick up this book. Maybe it was curiosity about my story, or maybe you're going through a struggle right now yourself. Whether your struggle is mental, physical or a combination of both, I want you to know you can always come out of it. At no point are you stuck. Don't believe the lie that says being stuck means you're never going to be able to move forward in life. It's simply not true.

Maybe you feel stuck right now. But if you start to put the pieces back together as best you can, there is no way you're going to remain in the same place you are today. As human beings, we are meant to evolve, and we evolve best when we are challenged. I've overcome too many obstacles in my life to know that obstacles are not dead ends. They're just a chance to come back stronger and more resilient than ever before.

Think of yourself like a car. If a car runs out of gas, that doesn't mean the car is worthless. A car doesn't lose its value if there's no gas in the tank. When you put gas back in the tank, that car is going to move, and it's going to take you where you want to go when you push your foot down on the accelerator.

Whenever I've been depressed and fearful in my life, there was something I needed to do to put "gas back in my tank." There was something I needed to change. Until I made a change, I continued to be down and depressed.

I can't tell you what needs to change in your life. It could be something as simple as the food you eat, or it could be something bigger like your career or one of your relationships. Regardless of what it is, I hope my story will inspire you to not be afraid to make the changes you need to make to get what you want out of life. Setbacks are temporary. Don't let them define you. If you look at some of the most successful people in the world, they didn't get to where they are now by taking the easy road. They got to where they are now because they are fighters, and they never gave up. No matter what.

For example, look at Oprah. She started from absolutely nothing. She was dirt poor. She had no connections. No African American woman in the history of humanity had ever even accomplished what she set out to accomplish in her life. Now she's worth three billion dollars. Do you think she ever took "no" for an answer? There's no way.

Look at Tony Robbins. He grew up with just his mom around, and she was abusive. He left home when he was 17 years old, and he had to support himself as a janitor. Now he has a net worth of almost 500 million dollars. But it's not the money he's made that impresses me. It's his obsession with helping other people that means the most to me.

This is the same obsession that's inspired me to keep going when I've felt like quitting over the years. My drive is that I want to help other people, and I'm not going to give up on my dream to do that in the biggest way I possibly can.

Another person who inspires me is my mother. Even though we don't see eye to eye, she never looks at the negative side of anything. She always tries to look at the positive side of everything and be at peace. She's thankful for everything she has, and she's always been that way.
She deals with a lot of challenges I won't go into in this book, but she never gives up her peace. She never gives up her happiness. She's a fighter, too. Just like me.

I've done several speaking gigs since my accident, and people always ask me, "How did you do it? How did you get through everything you've experienced?" And the truth is everybody's journey is different. I can only tell the people who ask me this what has worked for me. I haven't made all the right choices in my life. I haven't done everything the simple, easy way.

    The only choice you can make to ensure your success, which is true across the board for every single person living on planet earth, is the choice to never, ever give up.

Shock Your Life Into Action

Setbacks are temporary. They are not dead ends. Every successful person must overcome obstacles in their life. Some of us face things that make us feel powerless and worthless, but that's not the truth of who we are. As human beings, we never lose our value. We can always start over. We start over whenever we make a change to our lives in order to create a better, happier life for ourselves and those around us. We might have to do this a million times in our life, and that's okay. The only way we can ever truly lose is by giving up.

"I don't know what you're doing or where you're going, but, Jesse—just keep going."

My Nurse

Chapter 16

Be an Unrealistic Fighter

When I was in the hospital recovering from my accident, there was a nurse there who inspired me to stay alive. She looked after me in every way. She was always there whenever I needed something, and she encouraged me in my darkest moments. Without her, I'm not sure I would have made it through my hospital stay.

She would hold my hand as I lay there in excruciating pain in the hospital bed staring out of my window at the city I had hoped was going to be place where my life was going to finally begin. She held my hand in those moments when I didn't even want to be alive anymore, and she told me, "Jesse, just keep breathing."

Whenever I stopped breathing, she would squeeze my hand tight until I started breathing again. She did this for me for weeks. She stood by my side, and she kept me going with her prayers and emotional support. I'll always be thankful she did this for me.

Recently, I went back to the hospital I spent so much time in, and this nurse was there. When she saw me, she said, "I can't believe I'm looking at you right now. I fought for you so hard, and I wanted you to live."

She cried while standing there looking at me. She told me she was so happy I was still alive. She said, "I don't know what you're doing or where you're going, but, Jesse—just keep going."

This nurse showed me what it means to be an unrealistic fighter. She showed me what it means to never give up hope, even when it seems like all hope is lost. I'll never forget this lesson she taught me.

I've always seen myself as a fighter, and I've always wanted to make a huge impact on other people's lives. I want to shine my light in a positive way so the world can be a better place when I leave it.

When I set goals for my life, I'm a little bit like a car with too much horsepower on a racetrack. I slide around a little bit—I crash and burn from time to time—but I always get there. I've failed more times in my life than I can count, but that's never stopped me from picking up the pieces and trying again.

THE SHOCK OF A LIFETIME

You might ask after reading this book, "Is there anything in your life that's gone according to plan?" And the answer is no, not really. But I'm not afraid of failure. It's true what they say that the only thing we have to fear in life is fear itself. Fear destroys more dreams than failure ever will.

People are often so scared to try something new. They don't want to be embarrassed in front of their friends and family. You know now that I've been embarrassed in my life more times than I can count. I've messed up, and I've been handed a raw deal so many times that it doesn't even affect me anymore.

I know that each time I fail, I get that much closer to success. I've suffered hardship and lost everything more times than I can count. I went from being an up-and-coming fitness model, to being a person that was too ashamed of my scars to take my shirt off in public. I went from being mocked and disapproved of by my own family, to being on TV telling my story to a nation-wide audience.

Throughout my journey, I've met so many incredible people who have inspired me to keep fighting, and I've met a lot of people who are hurting just as bad as I have hurt in the darkest moments of my life. It's the people who are really hurting that I want to talk to right now. Because you know my story. You know I haven't had it easy. You know I've been depressed, suicidal and suffered through a total loss of my identity. But this story isn't just about me, what I've gone through and where I'm at today.

This story is about so much more than that. This story is about the power that comes out of pain, the absolutely relentless drive of the human spirit to not only survive, but to thrive, and the transformation that can take place when one person decides they're never going to give up on a dream.

Whatever you want in life, have the courage to fight for it. God wants us all to succeed in a positive way. As long as you're still breathing, you can succeed. Don't be afraid of anything. No one can truly hold you back except yourself. Be an unrealistic fighter. Work towards your goals like nothing else matters. Be the person who inspires everyone around you. Push yourself to your limit.

Don't let the people who doubt you win. Prove them wrong. Most of all, pray often. If you're going through hell, keep going. I have no doubt that you will one day rise like a phoenix out of the ashes. If I can do it, you can, too.

Shock Your Life Into Action

I was blessed with unrealistic fighters on my side that saw me through to my recovery. One of them was my nurse when I was in the hospital. Through her, I've learned to never give up hope, even when it seems that all hope is lost. I lost everything that was important to me when I was burned, but I gained the perspective that I truly needed in order to succeed. I learned that nothing, not even the threat of death, can stand in my way. As long as I live, I hope to inspire people to go after big things in their lives, even when others say it's going to be impossible. I am a living example of the fact that nothing is impossible. I came out of the ashes stronger, wiser and more dedicated to living the life I was meant to live than I could have ever imagined.

I want to be remembered as an unrealistic fighter. A man who never quit. Being unrealistic was how I was able to get out of that hospital bed, get on national TV, and inspire others all over the world to keep fighting.

My question to you is this: how do you want to be remembered? It's time to be unrealistic and become the person you were intended to be.

JESSE SINK

Photo Gallery

The view I saw for many months in the hospital.

THE SHOCK OF A LIFETIME

One of my amazing nurses who saved my life.

JESSE SINK

Some of the nurses who brought me back to life.

THE SHOCK OF A LIFETIME

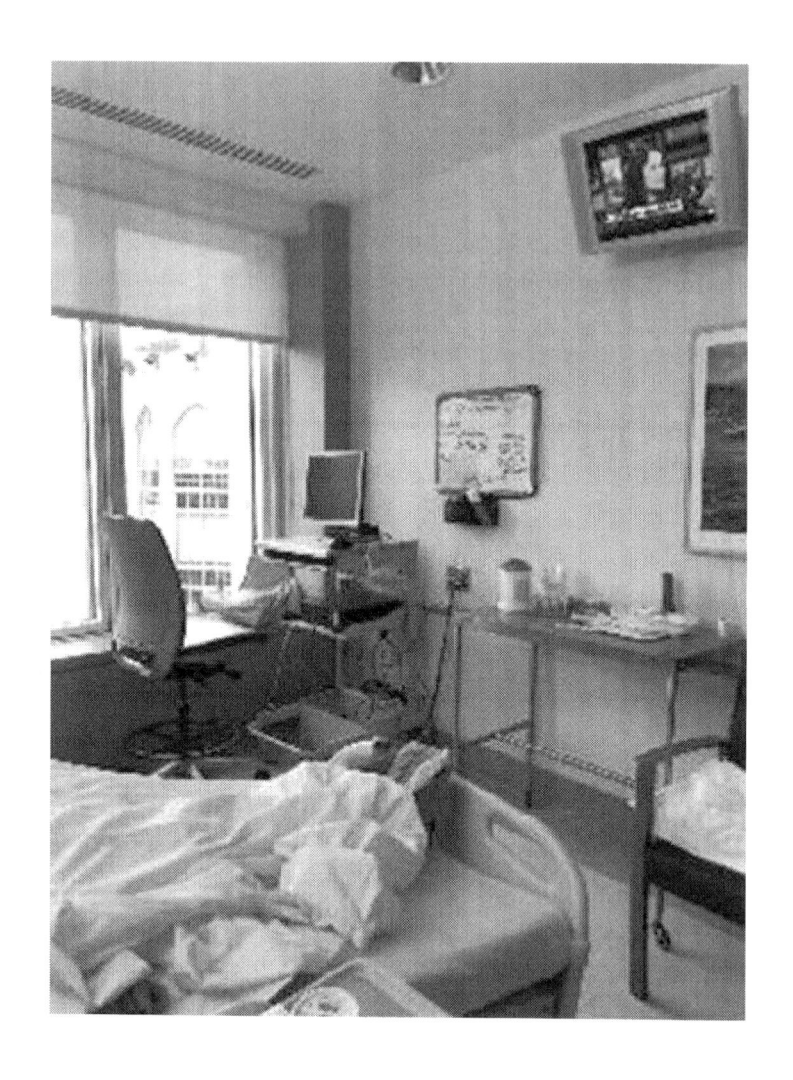

The room where I started my comeback.

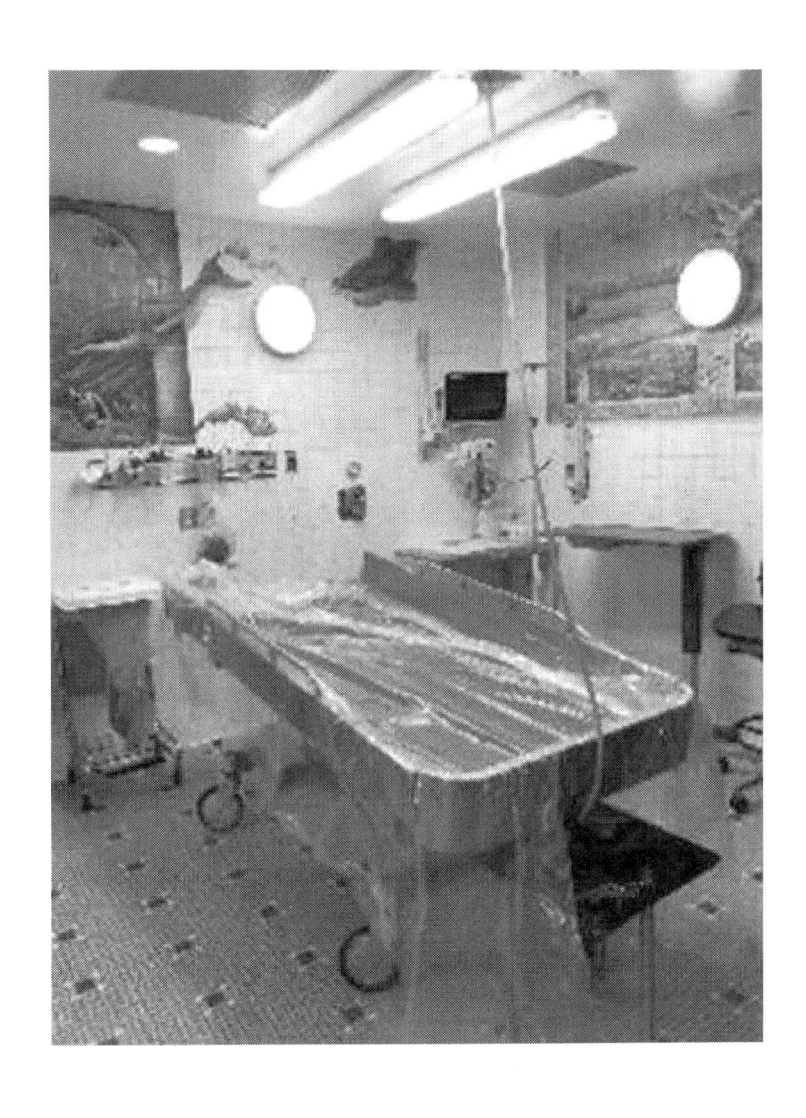

I was here, but I didn't die here.

About Jesse Sink

Jesse Sink is a model and fitness competitor who survived a deadly accident and is inspiring others with his story of tragedy and triumph.

In 2006, Jesse Sink was a 20-year-old fashion and fitness model in New York City when he woke up on top of a train at Penn Station. Moments later he was electrocuted, burned alive, and given two days to live.

JESSE SINK

After surviving 13, 800 volts, 2 months in a coma, and 13 surgeries – including arm amputation, skin grafting, vein re-routing and bone / muscle / tissue / nerve repair – Jesse Sink has re-learned how to walk, talk, write, and kick ass. Seven years after doctors deemed him "beyond repair," Jesse Sink is a fitness trainer, model, amateur bodybuilder and spokesperson in Los Angeles, inspiring others who are struggling to not just survive – but to thrive.

THE SHOCK OF A LIFETIME

BEFORE   AFTER

Just when you think life has you on your knees, you realize how blessed you are to be where you are in life.

No boundaries

THE SHOCK OF A LIFETIME

It was an honor to be a guest on The Doctors Tv Show

JESSE SINK

THE SHOCK OF A LIFETIME

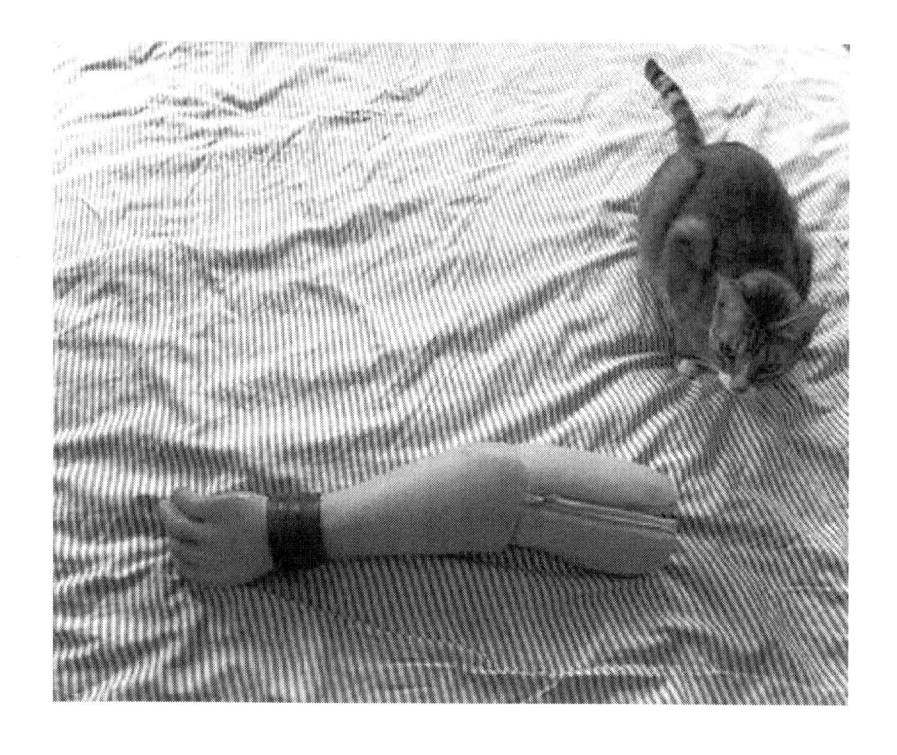

You are stronger than what is in front of you.

Shock your life into action and never look back.

Thank you so much for reading my book!

Let's connect on

&

I would love to hear from you.

@BionicJesse

www.BionicJesse.com

Made in the USA
Lexington, KY
28 August 2018